STO

ACPL ITEM
DISCARDED

P9-ECM-008

j523.47
Shepherd, Donna Walsh.
Uranus

4-95

ALLEN COUNTY PUBLIC LIBRARY
FORT WAYNE, INDIANA 46802

You may return this book to any location of
the Allen County Public Library.

DEMCO

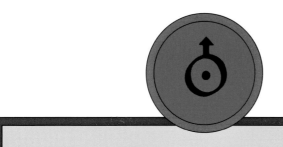

URANUS

DONNA WALSH SHEPHERD

URANUS

A FIRST BOOK
FRANKLIN WATTS
NEW YORK/CHICAGO/LONDON/TORONTO/SYDNEY

Allen County Public Library
900 Webster Street
PO Box 2270
Fort Wayne, IN 46801-2270

Cover photograph copyright © NASA

Photographs copyright © NASA: pp. 10, 12 left, 15, 19, 22, 25, 26, 31, 34, 37, 39, 42, 45, 47, 50, 52, 57; The Bettmann Archive: p. 12 right; The Royal Observatory Edinburgh/D. Malin: p. 17; Finley Holiday Films: p. 29.

Library of Congress Cataloging-in-Publication Data

Walsh Shepherd, Donna.
      Uranus / by Donna Walsh Shepherd.
          p. cm. — (First book)
      Includes bibliographical references and index.
      ISBN 0-531-20167-8
          1. Uranus (Planet) — Juvenile literature. [1. Uranus (Planet)]
I. Series
QB681.S55 1994
523.4′7—dc20   93-6097   CIP   AC

Copyright © 1994 Donna Walsh Shepherd
All rights reserved
Printed in the United States of America
6 5 4 3 2 1

CONTENTS

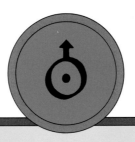

ACKNOWLEDGMENTS

Many thanks to all those who helped educate me and those who reviewed this manuscript. A special thanks to the good people of the Smithsonian Air and Space Research Library and the Jet Propulsion Laboratory, especially to Dr. Ellis Miner, who so graciously spent time with me and answered so many basic questions with such good humor.

This is dedicated to my mother and father, Bernice and Maurice Walsh, who, when I was a child, woke me in the middle of the night and took me outside to look at the stars.

DISCOVERING URANUS: OUR SEVENTH PLANET

CHAPTER ONE

Far from Earth in the dark sky, the mysterious blue planet, Uranus, circles the sun. Clouds, moons, and rings accompany this strange planet on its rounds nearly 2 billion miles (3.02 billion km) from the sun. Only those with the sharpest eyes who know exactly where to look in the night sky can see Uranus without a *telescope*. Even then, it looks more like a dim white star than a blue planet.

In 1781, everyone believed that Uranus was a star so far away you could barely see it. Then our *solar system* was the sun and six planets: Mercury, Venus, Earth, Mars, Jupiter, and Saturn. Beyond that were stars and space and nothing more.

Some of the secrets of cloudy Uranus were revealed by *Voyager 2* on its trip through the outer reaches of the solar system.

William Herschel, a German musician living in England, thought differently. He believed the sky held secrets, secrets he wanted to know. One day Herschel borrowed a telescope from a friend to look at Venus, but the telescope's foggy and fuzzy image frustrated Herschel. He decided to build a better one.

Although he could not quit his job as a musician, he began to build his own telescope in his spare time. As he worked, he became passionate about astronomy. After nearly two hundred failures, he finally produced a good, working telescope with a 6.5-inch (16.5-cm) reflecting mirror that showed clear images.

For his first project with his new, high-powered telescope, he decided to review what he already knew about the night sky. Each night through his telescope he watched the planets, stars, and comets that he knew so well to see if he could learn anything more about them. On March 13, 1781, he looked at a dim white star in the *constellation* Gemini and saw it was actually large and a pale blue color. Its size suggested to him that it was closer to Earth than anyone had thought and not part of Gemini at all.

Left: Sir William Herschel, originally a musician, became fascinated with astronomy. He built his own telescope and discovered Uranus. Right: A drawing of Herschel's great telescope. At first, the inventor and his sister thought they had discovered a new comet, not a planet.

Herschel excitedly believed that he had found a new comet. Assisted by his sister, Caroline, he began to record the movements of the comet. Soon, he and Caroline realized his new comet didn't behave like a comet. It moved slowly and had no tail. Many *astronomers* studied and measured the movements of the "comet." Finally they agreed it was not a comet at all. Herschel had discovered a new planet, the seventh known planet orbiting our sun. It was the first planet to be discovered since our ancient ancestors first charted the sky.

After everyone agreed a new planet had been found, they disagreed over what to name it. Herschel wanted to name it Georgium Sidus, after England's King George III. Some people called it Herschel after its discoverer. But tradition held. This planet, like the other six, was named for a god in Greek mythology. Even Earth is sometimes called Gaea, after the goddess that gives life. Because it orbited just beyond Saturn, the new planet was named Uranus for the god of the sky who fathered Saturn. Uranus was also the husband of Gaea, but later they separated which explained to our ancient ancestors why Earth was separate from the sky.

The discovery of Uranus through a telescope marked the beginning of a new age in astronomy. The Herschels continued to build bigger and better telescopes and to explore the night sky. Today, men and women are as eager to discover the secrets of the universe as William and Caroline Herschel were. Like the Herschels, they work hard to invent new equipment to help us find answers. Now technical equipment such as telescopes, computers, radio wave receivers, many kinds of cameras, and unmanned space probes assist us in gathering information and learning more.

Most of our new knowledge about Uranus was sent back by *Voyager 2*, a United States space probe designed and built by an international team of scientists to study the solar system. It took pictures and measurements of our solar system for years, sending them back to Earth by radio waves. Here our scientists and computers unlocked many of the secrets of Uranus by analyzing *Voyager's* information. They also discovered many with new questions to ask. *Voyager 2* will continue to travel farther and farther from Earth until it leaves the solar system for deep space. Even then, it will to send back messages of all it sees and hears.

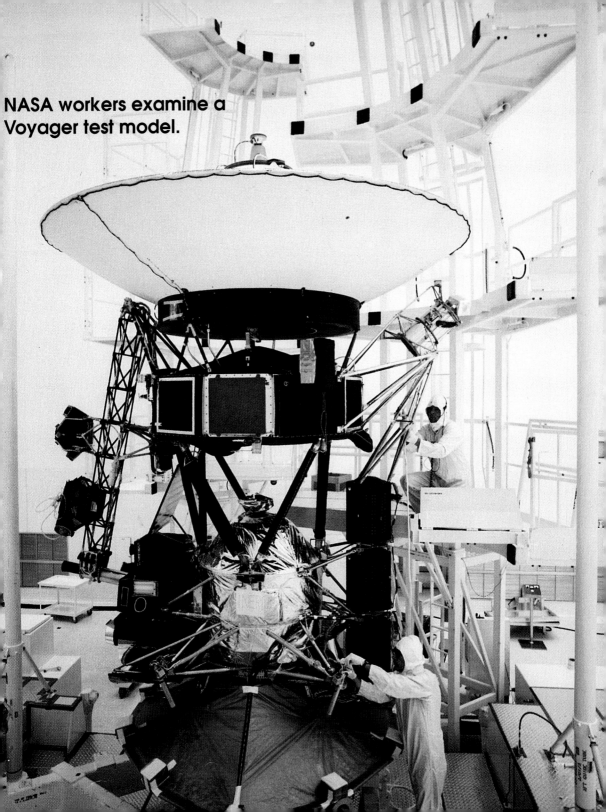

NASA workers examine a
Voyager test model.

THE SIDEWAYS PLANET

CHAPTER TWO

As our universe exploded into being, gases, liquids, and solids came swirling together, giving birth to galaxies that spread across the far-flung skies. Each *galaxy* is made up of many billions of stars. Our sun is a medium-size star in the Milky Way galaxy. Around the sun a family of planets formed. These nine planets and their moons make up our solar (sun) system. The solar system also contains *asteroids*, comets, and meteors, which orbit the sun. Earth is the third planet from the sun. Uranus is seventh. This system is our home in the heavens. Our galaxy is so large that as we begin exploring the solar system, it is like exploring our backyard.

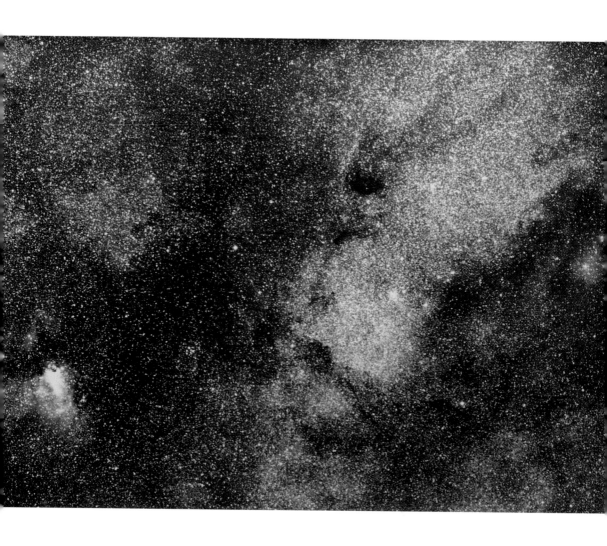

Our solar system, made up of nine planets
and the sun, is but a very small part of the
Milky Way galaxy.

Like all the other giant planets in our outer solar system (Jupiter, Saturn, and Neptune), Uranus is made of a swirl of gas, liquid, and solids. It has no solid surface to stand on. The solids, mostly silicon, iron, and a basalt-like rock, have settled into the center of the planet. The center of Uranus is a solid core about the size of Earth.

At the outer edge of the core, the solid elements mix with the great ocean that surrounds the rocky heart of the planet. This ocean is about 5,000 miles (8,000 km) deep. The deepest part of Earth's oceans is only about 7 miles (11 km) deep. Scientists think Uranus's ocean is mostly water, perhaps mixed with a bit of liquid ammonia and methane. The amazing thing about Uranus's ocean is that it is extremely hot — as hot as 8,000°F (14,430°C). Scientists think perhaps this great ocean was formed by icy comets that got caught and absorbed by Uranus. The force of the comets hitting Uranus was so great, it caused them to melt.

At the surface of this superheated ocean, the water vaporizes and mixes with a thick gaseous layer about 4,000 to 5,000 miles (6,400 to 8,000 km) deep. This layer of atmos-

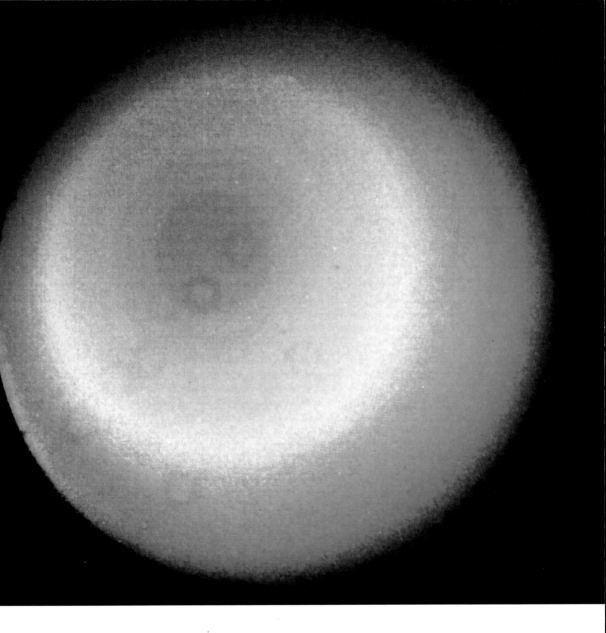

This photo of Uranus, which has been
computer-enhanced, was taken by *Voyager 2* from
a distance of 5.7 million miles (9.5 million km).

phere is mostly liquid hydrogen, methane, and some helium. The methane gas gives Uranus its blue-green color. No dividing line exists between the ocean and the atmosphere. One gradually turns into the other. Scientists wanted to determine exactly where the surface of Uranus was in the mass of liquid and gas that surrounds the solid heart of the planet. They decided that the surface of all the giant planets is where the atmospheric pressure is the same as Earth's atmospheric pressure at sea level. Above the gas layer is a layer of haze similar to our atmosphere, but it is made up of mostly hydrogen and helium.

The heavy gas layer pushes down on the superheated ocean with such force that the ocean water doesn't boil. Normally water on Earth boils at 212° F (100° C). On Uranus, the pressure from the gas layer has caused the ocean to become electrically charged. The movement of currents at the surface of the electrically charged ocean creates a magnetic field around the planet. This requires pressure millions of times greater than that at Earth's surface.

Earth and other planets in our solar system also have magnetic fields. Earth's magnetic field is created from its molten iron center that carries electricity. A magnetic field turns the planet into a giant magnet. That's why on Earth a compass will always point north. It is pointing to Earth's north magnetic field.

Here on Earth, and on most planets, the magnetic field lies close by the poles or the point of *axis* (turning). Uranus's field is 60 degrees off its point of axis. If Earth's field was 60 degrees off the axis, the compass needle might point to Los Angeles rather than to the North Pole.

As the solar wind from the sun blows by the planets to the edge of our solar system, it blows the charged particles from Uranus's magnetic field out behind the planet. This gives the planet an invisible, electrically charged magnetic tail. All planets with magnetic fields have magnetic tails. Because Uranus's rotation is at a different angle from its magnetic field, the solar wind blows the tail into an unusual corkscrew shape. As Uranus rotates, the tail twists and turns.

As most planets *orbit* the sun, they rotate, creating days and nights as each side of the planet turns to and then away from the sun. Earth does this. Uranus does not. Instead, it

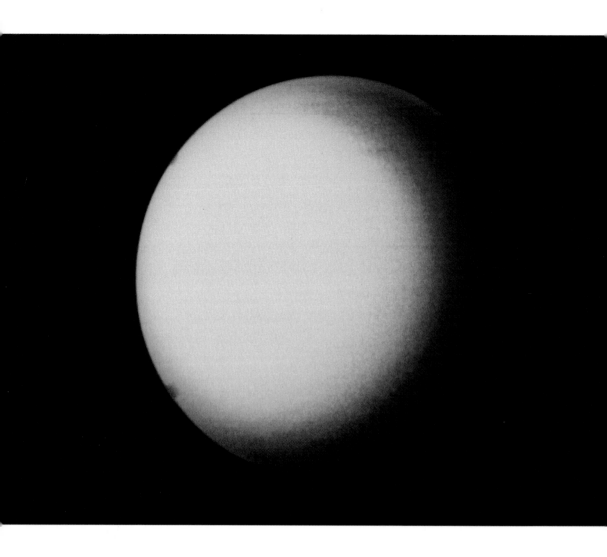

An entire view of the smooth surface of
Uranus, as seen through a special filter

seems almost as though Uranus has fallen over onto its side. The poles are not on the top and bottom of the planet like Earth's North and South poles, but rather on the sides, nearly where we would expect the equator to be. The planet spins from north to south, or top to bottom, instead of west to east the way Earth does. Uranus takes 17.25 hours to spin around completely, what we call a day on Earth. Scientists think that perhaps when Uranus was a young planet it was hit by a large asteroid, about the size of Earth, and was knocked over onto its side. Now Uranus tilts at 98 degrees off center, the straight up-and-down line. Earth tilts 23 degrees off center.

Uranus travels an oval path around the sun, speeding through space at 4.25 miles (7 km) every second, one fourth the speed of Earth. Still, because Uranus is so far from the sun, it takes eighty-four Earth years to complete one orbit, one Uranus year. Because the east and west hemispheres of Uranus don't rotate away from the sun, each face of Uranus faces light from forty-two Earth years as the planet moves through its eighty-four year orbit. Each of the four seasons lasts for twenty-one Earth years on Uranus.

Through a telescope Uranus appears as a pale bluish green beach ball. The smooth surface of Uranus means there are no surface storms that our telescopes and cameras can see. Bands of strong winds blow across Uranus's cloud surface as fast as 374 miles (599 km) per hour, but these winds blow the same way Uranus rotates. They don't disturb the atmosphere the way circular storms do, like the hurricanes and cyclones found on other planets. No one knows why we don't find these storms on Uranus.

Sunlight is dim on Uranus, dim and cold. The average surface temperature is a chilly −350° F (−216° C). Surprisingly, there is little difference in surface temperature between the side of the planet facing the sun and the side turned away from it.

The other giant planets have some kind of internal heat source. More heat radiates from them than can be explained by the sun's heat that shines on them. This doesn't happen on Uranus. Little heat escapes from it. Perhaps the smooth, thick, heavy atmosphere acts like a blanket, holding the heat in the ocean.

Like all the outer giant planets, Uranus has rings, at least eleven thin, dark rings. Because

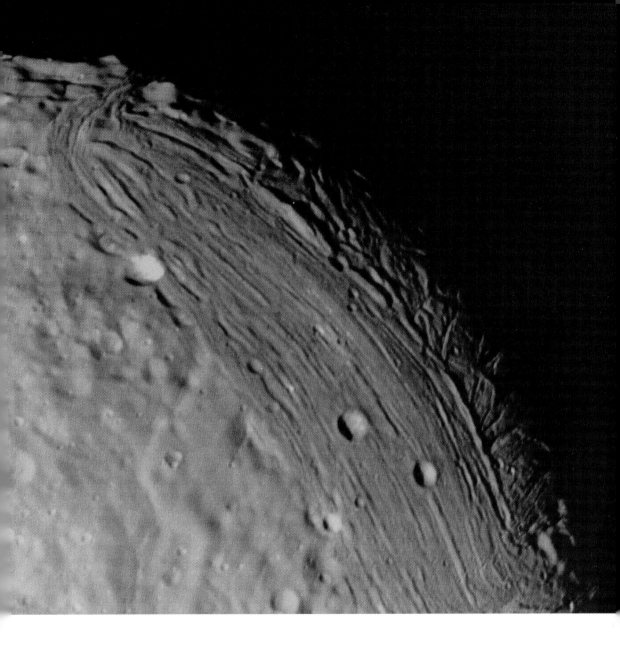

During its expedition, *Voyager 2* came closest to Miranda, the innermost and smallest of Uranus's major moons.

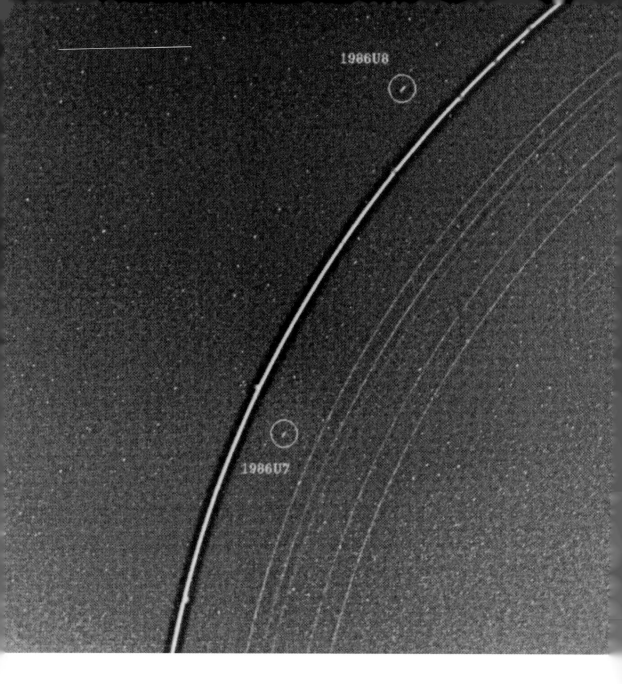

Rings and shepherding moons

Uranus rotates nearly on its side, the rings have formed circling the planet from top to bottom, instead of around, like Saturn's rings.

And like all the planets, except Mercury and Venus, Uranus has moons, fifteen of them. Five of the moons are large and were first studied through telescopes from Earth. These moons have some of the most interesting geology found anywhere in our solar system. The ten smaller moons were discovered by the *Voyager 2* spacecraft. They are all found in the bands of rings, and are called shepherding moons because their gravity keeps the rings in place.

Although *Voyager 2* greatly increased our knowledge about this strange blue planet, it also gave us much more to wonder about.

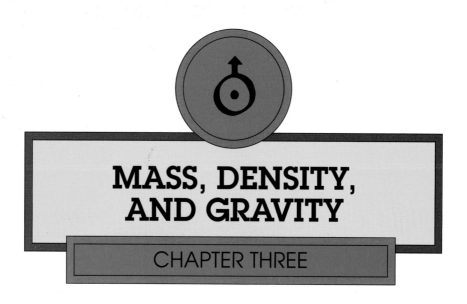

MASS, DENSITY, AND GRAVITY

CHAPTER THREE

There are many ways to measure things. When we measure planets we don't just measure their size. We also measure the mass, density, and *gravity* of the planets. To understand what these measurements mean, we compare them to the mass, density, and gravity of Earth.

The size of a planet is how much space it takes up. This is also called its volume. Sixty-three Earths could fit into one Uranus. The diameter of Uranus is 31,763 miles (51,118 km), four times greater than Earth's. Uranus is the third largest planet in our solar system. Only Jupiter and Saturn are larger.

Our solar system except Pluto:
(from top to bottom) Mercury, Venus,
Earth and its moon, Mars, Jupiter,
Saturn, Uranus, and Neptune

Even though Uranus is much larger than Earth in volume, it is made up of only 14.5 times more material than Earth. The material, or matter, that makes up a planet is called its mass. Uranus's mass includes the rocky core, the deep ocean, and the gaseous atmosphere. How can a planet that is sixty-three times larger than Earth have only 14.5 times more mass? This can be explained by the planet's density. Density is how tightly the mass, or material, is packed together. The material that makes up Earth is packed much tighter than the material that makes up Uranus.

A 4-inch (10-cm) ball of stone weighs far more than a 4-inch (10-cm) foam ball. This is because the *molecules* of stone are packed tightly together, while the foam ball has a good deal of weightless air space. Although both balls are the same size, the stone ball has greater mass, density, and weight.

A 1-pound (0.5-kg) ball of stone fits nicely into your hand, but a 1-pound (0.5-kg) foam ball is huge. They both have the same mass, 1 pound worth of material, but because the foam molecules are packed so much more loosely, less densely than the stone molecules, the same amount of material takes far more

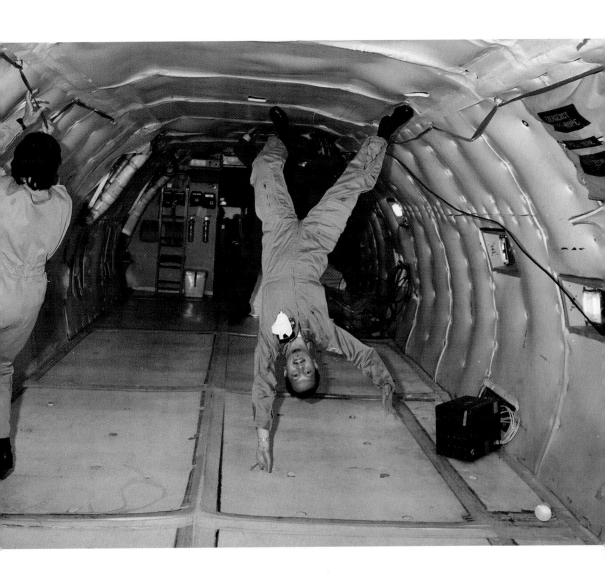

Space shuttle specialists train for the
weightlessness of outer space aboard a
specially equipped jet airplane.

space. The foam ball has a much lower density. It is the same with Earth and Uranus, which, just like the foam ball, has a lot of weightless air space.

We measure density compared to water. Because so much of Uranus is liquid or gas, the overall density of the planet is low compared to a rock planet of the same size. Uranus's average density is 1 1/4 times that of water. Earth's density is 5 1/2 times greater than water. Earth is the densest of the planets in our solar system.

Mass and density together influence gravity. Gravity is the force that pulls things toward a body's center. All things in space have a gravitational pull. This power can range from very weak to very strong. The base measurement of gravity on Earth is one. Earth's gravity keeps us all securely on Earth. Without gravity we'd just float away.

Gravity is slightly weaker on Uranus than on Earth. Gravity on Uranus is 0.91, or 91 percent of Earth's gravity. That means on the surface of Uranus, you would weigh less than you do on Earth. If you weigh 100 pounds (45 kg) on Earth, you would weigh 91 pounds (41 kg) on Uranus.

THE RINGS OF URANUS

In 1977, a group of scientists tried to measure the exact diameter of Uranus. They planned to do this by studying how long it took for the planet to pass in front of a specific star. From several places on Earth they watched Uranus come near the star, even through a telescope on an airplane. As they watched, the scientists were surprised to see the star blink out for a moment. It blinked again and again, five times in all. Then it passed out of view behind Uranus. What could cause this blinking, the scientists wondered. They were afraid that at this most important time, their equipment wasn't working correctly.

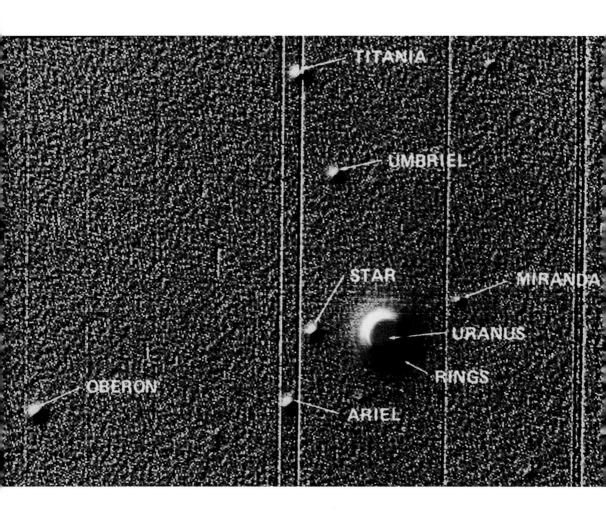

A computer-enhanced photo of
Uranus, its rings, and satellites taken
from an observatory on Earth

As the star came out from behind Uranus, it blinked out and blinked out again. On this side of Uranus, it blinked out at exactly the same distance from the planet and for the same length of time as it had on the other side of Uranus, five times in all. Then the scientists knew. Uranus has rings. Until then scientists thought only Saturn had rings.

William Herschel suspected Uranus might have rings. He spent a long time studying it through a much stronger and better telescope than his original one. Finally, he decided that there were no rings and the faint arc he saw must be a reflection from errors in the shape of the mirror's curve. He was probably right about the reflection. The rings are too dark and thin to be seen easily through telescopes from Earth, even now.

Voyager 2 has shown that all the giant planets have rings. Uranus has eleven rings that circle the planet from top to bottom. However, because Uranus's thin, dark rings were hard even for *Voyager 2* to see clearly against the black sky, scientists suspect there are more undiscovered rings, and parts of rings called arcs, circling Uranus. We have named the known rings for letters of the Greek alphabet.

Because all the rings are the same flat, dark color, scientists think the ring particles may be coated with something. Perhaps the dark color comes from black carbon that could be coating the rocks and ice that make up the rings. Perhaps it is methane gas that darkens with age and radiation. Or, perhaps, it is something else we now know nothing about.

Saturn's rings are very bright and easy to see, so it is puzzling why Uranus's rings are so dark. Saturn's rings contain ice and dust particles which reflect light. The darkened ice in Uranus's rings reflects very little light; only 5 percent of the dim sunlight that shines on the rings is reflected back.

Uranus's rings are made mostly of dirty ice boulders about 3 feet (1 m) across. Lanes of dust float nearby, but Uranus's rings have little dust in them. Scientists think there used to be dust in the ring system, but Uranus's gravity is pulling the dust into the planet, leaving only the larger, heavier boulders to form rings. Even these heavier rings are probably spiraling into the planet and eventually the rings

A photo from *Voyager 2* of Uranus's
rings with backlit dust particles

37

may disappear altogether. The lack of dust and small particles in Uranus's rings makes scientists believe that planetary rings may be only temporary. Even Saturn's large, brilliant rings may disappear into the planet in a few million years.

To get the best pictures and measurements of the rings, *Voyager 2* took the pictures looking back through the rings toward the sun and a star. Computers measured their size by how much starlight passed through the rings. The rings are very narrow and flat. The widest part of Uranus's largest ring, the outermost and brightest ring called the epsilon ring, is only 60 miles (96 km) across. Most of the others are only 1 to 2 miles (1.6 to 3.2 km) across, and many are not even a half mile (800 m) deep. The distance between the rings varies from 208 miles (335 km) to 1,784 miles (2,872 km).

For these boulders to stay in ring formation, there must be a force to hold them in place. The material in the rings is kept from floating away by the confining force of shepherding moons. A moon on each side of the ring has a gravitational pull that holds the ring in line. These moons seem to be made of the same

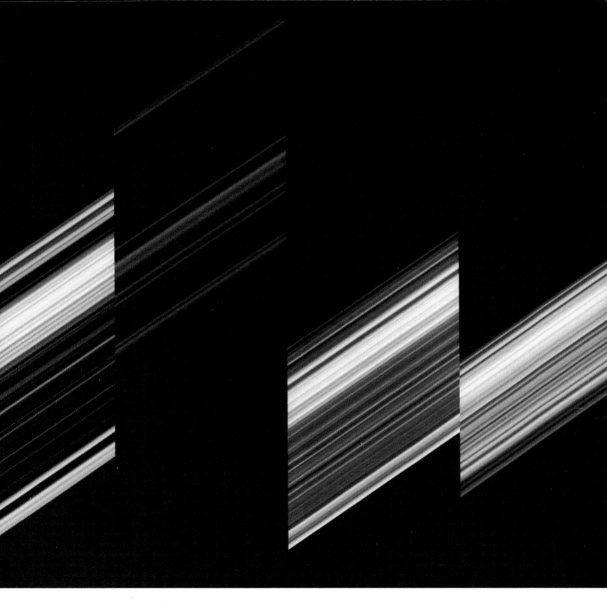

A computer-generated image of four slices of the epsilon ring around Uranus. The reddish areas represent the parts of the ring with less material, the yellow ones, more material. The true ring colors are very dark.

material as the rings and are the same flat, dark color. Possibly, the rings are made of old shattered moons. Because the dark rings and shepherd moons are so hard to see against the black sky, scientists believe more shepherd moons will be discovered by future space probes, both in the known rings and in any new rings that may be discovered.

THE MOONS OF URANUS

As Earth has its moon, Uranus also has moons. In 1787, William Herschel discovered the first two moons through his telescope. Years later, other astronomers discovered three more.

Scientists suspected that on *Voyager 2's* close encounter with Uranus it would find even more moons, or satellites. And it did. The close-up photos of Uranus showed ten more moons astronomers had not been able to see through telescopes from Earth. Most of these new moons are quite small, from 35 to 110 miles (56 to 177 km) across. They were all found in the ring belt located between the five larger moons and the planet.

These little moons appear to be made of the same dark, icy material as the rings. They

This drawing is based on a computer simulation of the *Voyager 2* encounter with Uranus.

have about the same density as water and may be frozen water, which is commonly found in the outer solar system. The new moons don't rotate; instead they continually hold the same face toward Uranus.

Perhaps these little moons were once a larger moon that broke apart. Now the pieces have been caught in the gravitational orbit of Uranus just as their own gravity keeps the ring material in formation. They are called shepherding moons because they shepherd the boulders that make up Uranus's rings into circular groups, just as dogs help shepherd sheep into groups. A moon on one side of the ring pulls the boulders toward it. A moon on the other side pulls them in that direction. The opposing forces of the moons keep the rings caught in the center.

Throughout our solar system, all the planets and moons have been named for Greek and Roman gods of mythology. Only Uranus is different. Here the moon names come from literature, from characters in William Shakespeare's plays and Alexander Pope's poetry.

About the same time the ten new Uranian moons were discovered, the United States space program suffered a tragic loss. The space shuttle *Challenger* exploded just after launch, killing the seven astronauts and a schoolteacher on board. Many wanted to name the new moons after these people.

These were not the first deaths to happen while exploring space. Other American astronauts and several Soviet cosmonauts have also been killed. These people have craters on Earth's moon named for them. Because our solar system belongs to all nations the International Astronomical Union, which names the features of space, thought it best to hold with tradition. Moon craters were named after the *Challenger* crew, and the newly discovered Uranian moons, like the older moons, were named for characters in literature. These new moons were named after women in Shakespeare's plays.

The *Voyager 2* cameras revealed many surprises besides ten new moons. On the five larger moons, they discovered some of the most varied and surprising land formations found anywhere in our solar system. Although we now know much more about these five moons, Miranda, Ariel, Umbriel, Titania, and Oberon, unfortunately *Voyager 2* was able to take pictures of only the south face of each moon. Their north faces remain a dark secret.

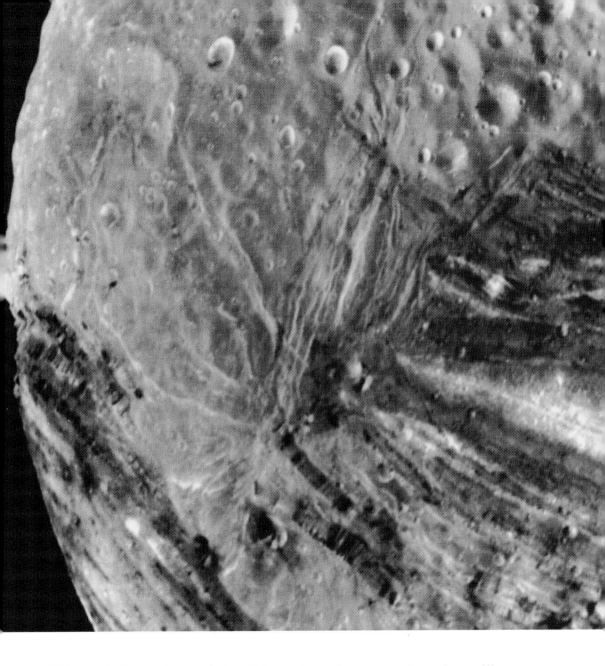

Miranda's patchwork of terrains, from craters to rolling
land, makes it the most unusual of Uranus's moons.

MIRANDA

Of the five larger moons, Miranda is the smallest and closest to the rings and to Uranus itself. *Voyager 2* flew nearest to it. Scientists didn't expect much from the little moon, barely 300 miles (480 km) across. When the pictures came in from *Voyager 2*, the scientists were stunned. Nowhere in our universe had they seen such diverse and unique landforms in such a small area. There are four separate areas of unusual landforms on Miranda's surface never before seen together.

Miranda bears the scars of a very active and violent past. Its land has been lifted and twisted. Canyons and faults turn and cross each other. Ice floes arc across the surface. Ribbons of land bend and ripple, forming huge ovals and deep Vs. The entire moonscape has been pockmarked by craters. New ridged land formations lie next to old weathered rolling land.

To many people the oddest thing on this odd moon is the "racetrack," an oval-shaped series of side-by-side grooves. These grooves are cliffs 12-miles (19-km) high. Even Mount Everest on Earth is only 7-miles (11-km) high, and it is a high

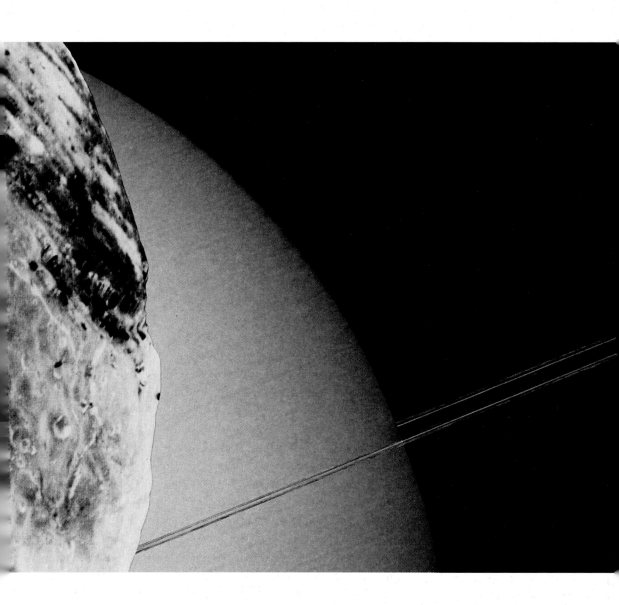

This composite photo shows Uranus
as seen from Miranda.

point on a high plateau, not straight down like the cliffs of Miranda. These cliffs are so high that if you stood on top of one and dropped a rock, it would take ten minutes to reach the ground.

What could have been the cause of Miranda's strange land formations and violent past? One theory is that the moon broke apart, perhaps after colliding with a large comet, and when it pulled back together some of the pieces came back turned inside out. The land that had been on the inside of the moon was now on the outside, and the old weathered outside was now in the center of the planet. Scientists also think that there has been a great deal of melting and freezing on Miranda. As it melted, the lighter material rose to the surface, and the heavier elements sank to the inside of the moon. Or maybe liquid ammonia and water in the moon's interior seeped through cracks to the surface, then froze. Whatever forces created Miranda, certainly created a strange little moon.

ARIEL

Ariel orbits next to Miranda. It is 720 miles (1,150 km) across. Like Miranda, it appears to be made of frozen water and gases. Ariel's active history is written on its face. It is pitted with craters and crossed with faults. Some of these faults have been filled in as liquids flowed to the moon's surface and froze. These long faults could have formed as Ariel froze, melted, and froze again. That would cause the moon's surface to expand, contract, and expand again, cracking as it did. Bright circles on Ariel's surface are icy crater rims. Most of these are small, only 3 to 6 miles (5 to 10 km) across, although one is 30 miles (50 km). Long ago Ariel and Miranda were named after characters in Shakespeare's play *The Tempest*. This is fitting because in the play a great storm changes the lives of the characters, just as forces of nature have changed these two moons.

UMBRIEL

Umbriel is the same size as Ariel, but quite different. Actually this old moon is different from all the other Uranian moons. It is very dark. Why Umbriel should be so much darker than the neighboring moons is a mystery. It does not have the active past of either Miranda or

Like Miranda, Ariel is made of ice and gases. The bright circles on this moon's surface are icy crater rims.

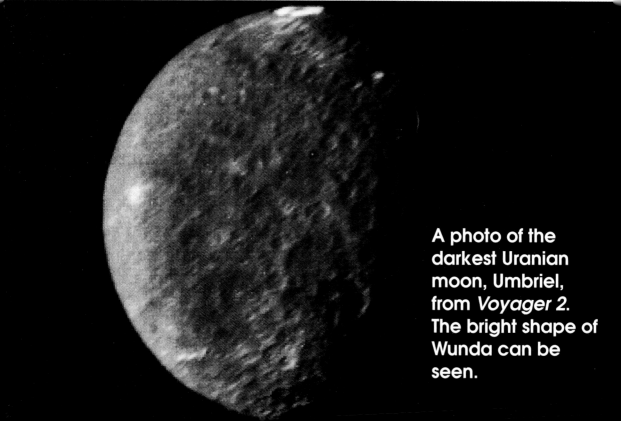

A photo of the darkest Uranian moon, Umbriel, from *Voyager 2*. The bright shape of Wunda can be seen.

Ariel. There are no cliffs and valleys, no ice floes, no twisting faults. Mostly Umbriel seems to have done little besides circle Uranus, grow dark, and be hit by asteroids. It is heavily marked with old craters, especially on the southern part of the moon.

Voyager 2's pictures of Umbriel face the south pole. At the top of the picture, on Umbriel's equator, is a large glowing white circle about 90 miles (145 km) across. It has been named Wunda. Because of the angle of the picture, it is hard to tell what Wunda could be. Most likely it is a new crater and the brightness comes from freshly exposed ice.

TITANIA

Only 980 miles (1,578 km) across, Titania is the largest of Uranus's moons. Like Ariel, this moon is streaked with faults and cracks, canyons and craters. Some of these faults stretch 1,000 miles (1,600 km) over the moonscape and are 45 miles (72 km) wide, about five times larger than our Grand Canyon. Bright white lines across the face of Titania probably come from sunlight reflected off frosty canyon walls. It appears that there still may be internal move-

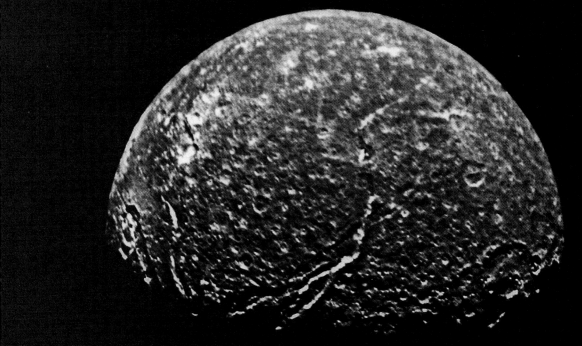

Uranus's biggest moon, Titania, has some faults more than five times the size of the Grand Canyon.

Sir Herschel discovered this moon of Uranus first and named it Oberon, after the fairy king in Shakespeare's *A Midsummer Night's Dream*.

ment within Titania; the moon may still be forming. Its surface and interior quake and shift, and liquids flow to the surface and freeze. At one time Titania must have had a partially molten center.

OBERON

Oberon is Uranus's outermost moon and just slightly smaller than Titania. It was the first of Uranus's moons to be discovered. William Herschel found it in 1787; shortly thereafter, he found Titania.

Oberon's surface is old and heavily marked with craters. It is a light-colored, icy moon, but many of its craters have dark floors. This could be caused by some kind of dark lava or liquid seeping up to the surface after the impact that formed the crater. In the middle of one crater is a mountain, about 12-miles (19-km) high. This is not a volcano, but rebound material. When a comet or asteroid hit Oberon, the molten lava shot back up toward the sky and solidified that way.

THE FUTURE

CHAPTER SIX

In the first two hundred years after Uranus was discovered, we learned little about the planet. It is just too far away from Earth to see in much detail, even with our best telescopes. That changed on January 24, 1986. In only a few hours, *Voyager 2* gathered enough information to increase our knowledge of Uranus many times over. We have learned exciting new truths we couldn't have begun to guess. We have also discovered many more puzzling new questions.

Before *Voyager 2* was launched in 1977, scientists had planned to send a whole series of space probes to explore and study the outer planets. They wanted to take advantage of the alignment of all four giants on the same side of the sun, a rare occurrence that wouldn't happen again for 175 years. They called this mission to the planets the Grand Tour. Unfortunately, government funding was cut and the mission was limited to two probes studying only Jupiter and Saturn.

The information these probes sent back was so exciting and valuable that in 1981 the government allowed the scientists to reprogram *Voyager 2*'s course and equipment so it would briefly fly by Uranus and then Neptune. The space probe used the gravity of each planet that it passed to fling it out at much greater speed toward the next planet. Using this gravity assist, it took *Voyager 2* eight and a half years to travel from Earth to Uranus. If we sent out a probe without any nearby planets to give it a boost, it would take thirty years to travel the same distance. Because the unplanned Uranus visit was arranged after *Voyager 2* was already launched, it spent less than one day at Uranus. The most important work was done in only a few hours with equipment not properly designed for Uranus's low light. Still, the results were spectacular.

Even though *Voyager 2* has now flown by all the outer planets except Pluto, which is not near *Voyager*'s path, it continues its work. Now the space probe is headed out into deep space looking for the edge of our solar system. Eight hours a day scientists listen to messages *Voyager 2* sends back as it hunts for the point where the solar winds die and charged ions no longer travel away from the sun, but rather toward it. This is the edge of our solar system.

A lack of money continues to force the U.S. space exploration program to move more slowly then we would like. No new space probes are planned for Uranus in this century. Because it takes several years to plan for a space probe, design it, build it, and send it to Uranus, it will be many years after the turn of the century before we are able to look for answers to all our puzzling new questions. Uranus, its secrets securely hidden under a thick, blue blanket of atmosphere, will remain a mystery circling through the dark sky nearly two billion miles away.

Although the visit to Uranus lasted only hours, *Voyager 2* was able to take this stunning farewell shot.

FACT SHEET ON URANUS

Symbol for Uranus —

Position — Uranus is the seventh planet from the sun. It is separated from Earth in the solar system by the planets Mars, Jupiter, and Saturn.

Rotation period — 17 hours, 8 minutes

Length of year — 1 year on Uranus is equal to 84 years (30,681 days) on Earth.

Diameter — 31,763 miles (51,138 km)

Distance from the sun (depending on location in orbit) — least: 1,702,100,000 miles (2,740,381,000 km); greatest: 1,870,800,000 miles (3,011,988,000 km)

Distance from Earth (depending on orbit) — least: 1,607,000,000 miles (2,587,270,000 km); greatest: 1,961,000,000 miles (3,157,210, 000 km)

Number of moons — 15 known moons. Scientists believe there may be more, as yet undiscovered, moons.

Number of rings — 11 known rings. Scientists believe there may be more, as yet undiscovered, rings and parts of rings.

Surface temperature — –357° F (–228° C).

Volume — 63 Earths

GLOSSARY

Asteroid — a small rocklike object found in our solar system

Astronomer — scientist who studies space and everything found in it

Axis — An imaginary line around which an object turns, or rotates

Comet — A ball of frozen gases and dust that has a large oval orbit around our sun or a star. Comets often have a tail caused by the solar wind blowing dust particles out behind the comet head.

Constellation — Eighty-eight recognized groupings of stars about which the ancients created stories

Crater — A round depression in the ground, usually made by an impact with a meteor or by a volcano

Galaxy — A very large group of billions of stars

Gravity — A force within an object that pulls other objects toward itself

Molecule — The smallest bit of something that has the same characteristics as the whole

Orbit — The path in which something continuously moves around something else

Radiation — Rays of heat, light, or energy traveling through space

Rotation — Turning or spinning around a center point

Satellite — Something that moves in an orbit around something larger. The moon is Earth's satellite and Earth is the sun's satellite.

Solar system — All the planets, their satellites, comets, and asteroids that orbit a sun

Space probe —A craft with specially designed equipment sent through space to explore and send back information, usually by radio wave. It may even land on a moon or planet.

Telescope — An instrument that makes things appear much closer and clearer by using lenses or mirrors to collect light and magnify its image

Universe — Everything that exists: Earth, other planets, sun, stars, galaxies, space

FOR FURTHER READING

Asimov, Isaac. *Uranus: The Sideways Planet*. Milwaukee: Gareth Stevens, 1988.

Branley, Franklyn M. *Uranus: The Seventh Planet*. New York: Crowell, 1988.

Darling, David J. *The Stars*. Minneapolis: Dillon Press, 1985.

Harris, Alan, and Paul Weissman. *The Great Voyager Adventure*. Englewood Cliffs, N.J.: Julian Messner, 1990.

Hunt, Gary and Patrick Moore. *Atlas of Uranus*. Cambridge, England: Cambridge University Press, 1989.

Maurer, Richard. *The Nova Space Explorer's Guide*. New York: Clarkson N. Potter, 1985.

Simon, Seymour. *Saturn*. New York: Morrow, 1985.

_____. *Neptune*. New York: Morrow, 1991.

INDEX

ABOUT THE AUTHOR

Donna Walsh Shepherd lives in Anchorage, Alaska, with her husband and three sons. Between traveling and writing books and magazine and newspaper articles, she teaches writing and literature at the University of Alaska Anchorage.